The World of Classical Music

A BOOK OF POSTCARDS
LIBRARY OF CONGRESS

Pomegranate Artbooks / San Francisco

Pomegranate Artbooks
Box 6099
Rohnert Park, CA 94927

ISBN 1-56640-958-6
Pomegranate Catalog No. A712

Pomegranate publishes books of postcards on a wide range of subjects.
Please write to the publisher for more information.
© 1994 Library of Congress

Cover designed by Mark Koenig
Printed in Korea

06 05 04 03 02   13 12 11 10 9 8 7 6

To facilitate detachment of the postcards from this book, fold each card along its perforation line before tearing.

*W*hile many people know that the Library of Congress is the largest library in the world, not as many are aware of its preeminence as a musical treasure-house. The Library's classical music collections encompass not only rare instruments and manuscripts but also books, periodicals and printed music ranging from seventeenth-century works to yesterday's copyright deposits. The Music Division's special collections typically serve as focal points of both research and further creative and interpretive endeavors.

The Library has also been a center for chamber music since the 1920s, when Elizabeth Sprague Coolidge created an endowment that commissioned works from many of the outstanding composers of our century, including Barber, Bartók, Copland, Schoenberg and Stravinsky. The legacy and attendant collections of Mrs. Coolidge and subsequent major patrons, such as Gertrude Clark Whittall and Serge Koussevitzky, continue to draw performers, scholars and music lovers alike to the Library in record numbers.

In this book of postcards, compiled from the collections of the Library of Congress, image follows fascinating image exploring the history of classical music: its composers, manuscripts, instruments and performers.

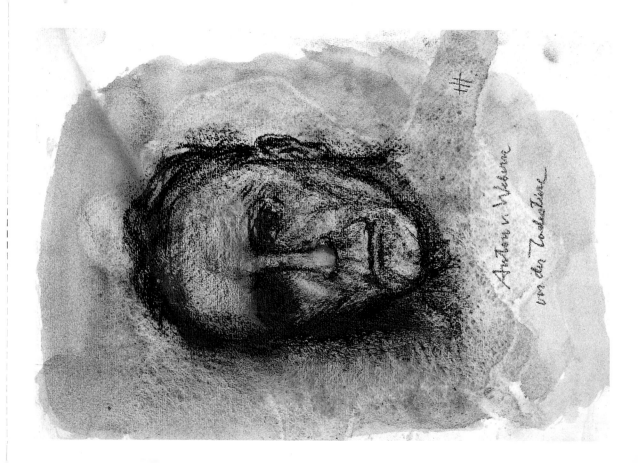

Anton in Wehern
vor der Todesbinn

The World of Classical Music

Anton von Webern (Austrian, 1883–1945) studied with Arnold Schoenberg and, with Alban Berg, further developed the theory of atonality and the practice of twelve-tone composition. This image of Webern is a sketch for a painting by Hildegard Jone, c. 1927.

Pomegranate, Box 6099, Rohnert Park, CA 94927

The World of Classical Music

Béla Bartók (1881–1945), Hungarian composer and major figure of twentieth-century music, was an avid student of folkways and folk music, and, like Dvořák, Kodály and others, he integrated them freely into "serious" forms. His String Quartet No. 5 was first performed in 1935 at the Library of Congress, where Bartók himself also performed after his arrival in the U.S. in 1940.

Pomegranate, Box 6099, Rohnert Park, CA 94927

The World of Classical Music

Few performers typify the highly charged artistic life as did Vladimir Horowitz (1903–1989), pictured here in New York in 1928, during his first American tour. Born in Ukraine, Horowitz was naturalized as an American citizen in 1942. His prodigious talent wore out every adjective, but Horowitz's disdain of interpretive orthodoxies made him a controversial figure throughout his career.

Pomegranate, Box 6099, Rohnert Park, CA 94927

Pomegranate, Box 6099, Rohnert Park, CA 94927

The World of Classical Music

A whimsical cartoon from the March 1906 edition of
Jugendblätter, a German children's magazine, showing
Ludwig van Beethoven (German, 1770–1827) directing a
celestial ensemble with characteristic intensity—and
clearly brooking no artistic compromise even in the
afterlife.

The World of Classical Music

Christopher Heckel's oil portrait of Ludwig van
Beethoven (German, 1770–1827) at age forty-five.

Pomegranate, Box 6099, Rohnert Park, CA 94927

The World of Classical Music

Legendary Italian violinist Niccolò Paganini (1782–1840) was perhaps the first musical superstar. Notwithstanding Paganini's spectacular virtuosity, his fame owed as much to an outsize personality and publicity machine as to musicianship.

Pomegranate, Box 6099, Rohnert Park, CA 94927

Das Gewandhaus
Allegro vivo
(Introduction aus Ali Baba)
an Fräulein
Henriette Grabau
zu freundlicher Erinnerung
Felix Mendelssohn Bartholdy
Leipzig 23/2 36

The World of Classical Music

Felix Mendelssohn (German, 1809–1847), like
Schoenberg and Gershwin, was a talented amateur artist
as well as a composer. He made this watercolor of the
Gewandhaus, the principal concert hall of Leipzig, in 1936
for the album of Henriette Grabau. The music below the
picture, also in Mendelssohn's hand, is from Cherubini's
Ali Baba.

Pomegranate, Box 6099, Rohnert Park, CA 94927

The World of Classical Music

Composer and pianist Percy Aldridge Grainger (1882–1961) was born in Australia, moved to Britain in 1900 and settled in the United States in 1914, becoming a citizen in 1919, around the time this photograph was taken by portraitist Pirie McDonald. Grainger's works as a whole are marked by a directness and originality that were much admired by such contemporaries as Delius.

Pomegranate, Box 6099, Rohnert Park, CA 94927

The World of Classical Music

Titled "Es ist das Heyl uns kommen her" (roughly, "Salvation Has Come"), Cantata No. 9 is one of some three hundred sacred cantatas composed early in the eighteenth century by Johann Sebastian Bach (German, 1685–1750). Bach's cantatas represent some of the most beautiful, virtuosic and inventive of all his writing.

Pomegranate, Box 6099, Rohnert Park, CA 94927

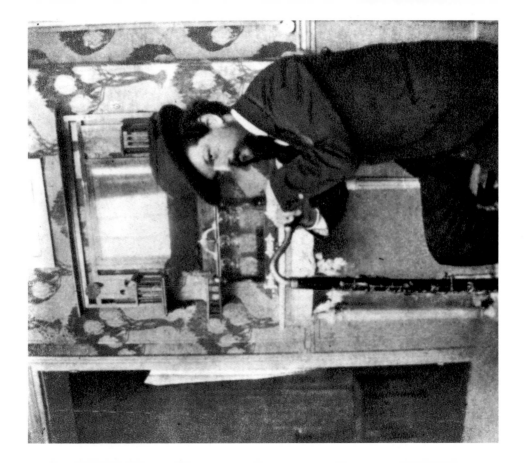

The World of Classical Music

Composer, conductor and critic Claude Debussy (French, 1862–1918) was a natural rebel who chafed at fame as much as at convention. While considered the originator and chief exponent of musical impressionism, Debussy abhorred the idea of leading any sort of "movement." This photograph was taken in 1909 by writer Pierre Louÿs, whose works were the narrative basis of Debussy's 1898 *Chansons de Bilitis*.

Pomegranate, Box 6099, Rohnert Park, CA 94927

The World of Classical Music

Aaron Copland (American, 1900–1990) in his studio in the
Berkshires, September 1946.

Pomegranate, Box 6099, Rohnert Park, CA 94927

Wolfgang Mozart

den 13 Merz 1770.

The World of Classical Music

Wolfgang Amadeus Mozart (Austrian, 1756 -1791) wrote
this letter to his sister, "Nannerl" (Maria Anna), when he
was fourteen years old and touring Italy with his father. It
contains news, chitchat and a postscript: "Kiss Mamma's
hands for me 1000000000000 times."

Pomegranate, Box 6099, Rohnert Park, CA 94927

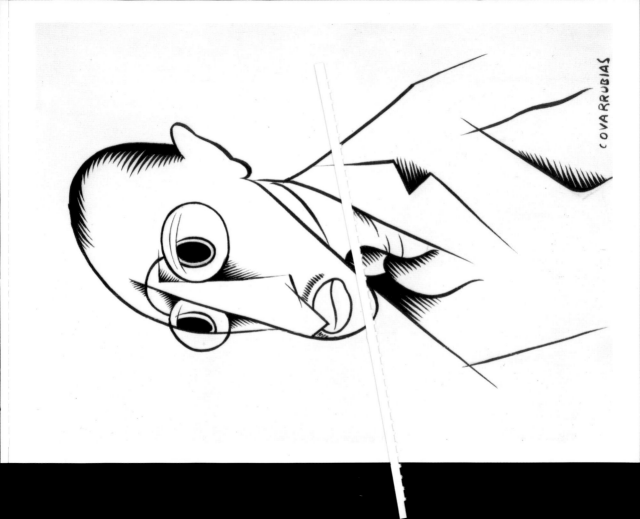

The World of Classical Music

A caricature of Russian-born American composer Igor
Stravinsky (1882–1971) by Miguel Covarrubias (Mexican,
1904–1957). Covarrubias, who went to New York in 1923
and worked there as an illustrator and theater designer for
some twenty years, gained renown as one of the most
penetrating caricaturists of any age.

Pomegranate, Box 6099, Rohnert Park, CA 94927

The World of Classical Music

Lili Boulanger (French, 1893–1918) learned to play the piano, cello, harp and violin as a child despite chronic ill health. At sixteen she turned to composition, and before her death nine years later she had composed some fifty works, including the cantata *Faust et Hélène* (1913), for which she was the first woman to be awarded the Prix de Rome.

Pomegranate, Box 6099, Rohnert Park, CA 94927

The World of Classical Music

The great Russian composer and pianist Sergei
Rachmaninoff (1873–1943) in rehearsal with the
Philadelphia Orchestra in the late 1930s, with
concertmaster Alexander Hilsberg at left and Eugene
Ormandy, who had recently inherited the conductorship of
Philadelphia from Stokowski, in the background at right.

Pomegranate, Box 6099, Rohnert Park, CA 94927

The World of Classical Music

Heitor Villa-Lobos (Brazilian, 1887–1959), captured by an unknown photographer in Rio de Janeiro in 1941.

Pomegranate, Box 6099, Rohnert Park, CA 94927

The World of Classical Music

Fritz Kreisler (1875–1962), born in Vienna, at seven was the youngest person ever to be admitted to the Vienna Conservatory. Despite brilliant work there and a respectable American tour afterward, he put down the violin for two years to serve in the armed forces and study medicine. Pictured here just before World War I, which interrupted his music career a second time, Kreisler went on to become one of the most celebrated violinists of the century; he became an American citizen in 1943.

Pomegranate, Box 6099, Rohnert Park, CA 94927

The World of Classical Music

This watercolor of a casual George Gershwin (American, 1898–1937) at the piano by Henry Botkin (b. 1896) was painted in the summer of 1934, when Gershwin was staying at Botkin's house on the South Carolina coast. Gershwin had retreated there to soak up the area's musical flavors as he began composing *Porgy and Bess*, based on the DuBose Heyward novel set in nearby Charleston.

Pomegranate, Box 6099, Rohnert Park, CA 94927

The World of Classical Music

Giacomo Puccini (1858–1924), superstar of a family of
distinguished musicians and, with Verdi, one of the most
highly regarded Italian opera composers, in an interesting,
molto mysterioso portrait made in 1907 by a photographer
named F. C. Bangs. The photograph was probably taken
in New York, where Puccini had visited that year to
attend a festival of his works at the Metropolitan Opera.

Pomegranate, Box 6099, Rohnert Park, CA 94927

The World of Classical Music

Title page, piano/vocal score, *La Nuit de Noel*, 1895.
Nikolai Rimsky-Korsakov (Russian, 1844–1908) began
composing this four-act opera in 1894, and it premiered a
year later in St. Petersburg. Based on a story by Gogol, it
features the magical, fantastic and exotic elements
characteristic of Russian ballet. Although this score was
published in Germany, its cover page is in Russian and
the interior is multilingual.

Pomegranate, Box 6099, Rohnert Park, CA 94927

The World of Classical Music

Remembered as a composer who overcame all manner of obstacles to make a lasting mark, a suffragist who conducted her "March of the Women" from a jail cell with her toothbrush, and a prolific literary raconteur of high style, Dame Ethel Smyth (English, 1858–1944) remains one of the singular personalities of her age. Her two best works, the Mass in D and the opera *The Wreckers*, garnered enduring critical admiration.

Pomegranate, Box 6099, Rohnert Park, CA 94927

The World of Classical Music

Gathered around a typically perfectly turned-out Maurice
Ravel (French, 1875–1937) at the piano are George
Gershwin (American, 1898–1937) and three other
attendees at a party thrown for Ravel's fifty-third birthday
in New York City during his 1928 American tour. The
year would see both composers create works of lasting
acclaim—Gershwin with *An American in Paris* and Ravel
with *Bolero*.

Pomegranate, Box 6099, Rohnert Park, CA 94927

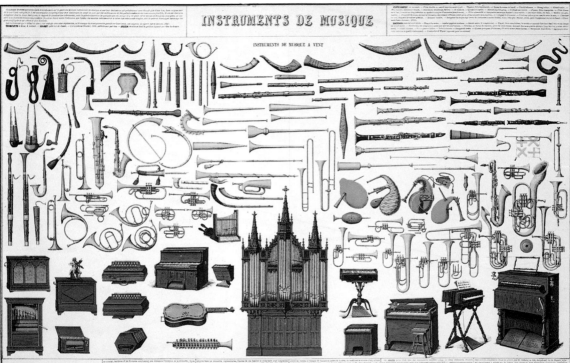

INSTRUMENTS DE MUSIQUE

INSTRUMENTS DE MUSIQUE A VENT

The World of Classical Music

This foldout chart of wind instruments from the *Encyclopédie Bouasse-Lebel* (c. 1860) depicts the principal instrument families, with examples from different ages; the straight horns at center, for example, had their demise with ancient Rome, while the valved brasses, keyed woodwinds and organs probably were taken directly from instrument makers' catalogs. Depictions of some older instruments range from less than accurate to downright fanciful.

Pomegranate, Box 6099, Rohnert Park, CA 94927

The World of Classical Music

La Bohème, by Giacomo Puccini (Italian, 1858–1924), is considered by many to be his masterpiece. The second act's incandescent melange of action and emotion is a highlight of the opera; here, the revelry, coquetry, jealousy and intoxication of new love seem almost to leap from the page of Puccini's holograph score.

Pomegranate, Box 6099, Rohnert Park, CA 94927

The World of Classical Music

Plate LII from *l'Art du Facteur d'Orgues* (Paris, 1770), a
monumental treatise on organ design and manufacture in
mid-eighteenth-century France compiled by Dom
François Bédos de Celles (1709–1779), a Benedictine
monk. The volume is illustrated with the extraordinary
engravings of Pierre Claude Delagardette (1743–1782).

Pomegranate, Box 6099, Rohnert Park, CA 94927

The World of Classical Music

Popular and influential French composer Charles Gounod (1818–1893) is remembered today largely for his *Faust* (1859), which brought him widespread fame and became one of the most successful French operas of the century.

Pomegranate, Box 6099, Rohnert Park, CA 94927

The World of Classical Music

Frontispiece from the portfolio *Parsifal, 15 Bilder zu Richard Wagner's Bühnenweihfestspiel*, by illustrator Franz Stassen (1869–1949), published in Berlin in 1901.

Pomegranate, Box 6099, Rohnert Park, CA 94927

PUCCINI IN EGYPT

The World of Classical Music

"Puccini in Egypt," drawing of Giacomo Puccini (Italian, 1858–1924) from *Caricatures by Enrico Caruso* (1914).

Pomegranate, Box 6099, Rohnert Park, CA 94927